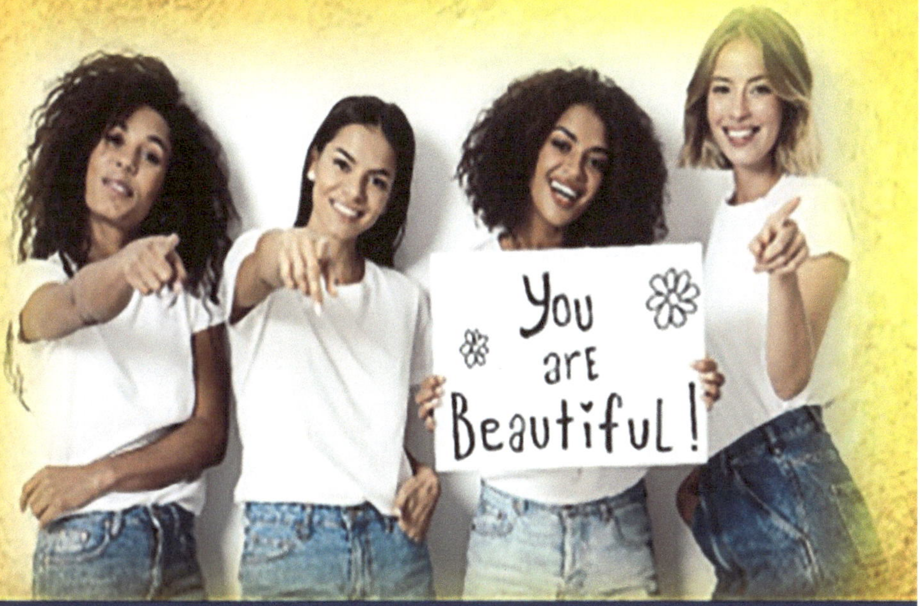

Urban Woman's Annual journal

2020
"The Year of Plenty"

THIS JOURNAL BELONGS TO:

_____

URBAN WOMAN'S ANNUAL JOURNAL

© Copyright 2019 by Averie Hatton

All Rights Reserved. No part of this book may be reproduced or transmitted in any form or by any means, electronic or mechanical, including photocopying, recording or by any information storage and retrieval system, without written permission from the publisher. Request for reproduction or related information should be addressed to the author.

Averie Hatton creates spiritual growth and personal development content for multimedia platforms and faith-based organizations.

Copies of this book and others are available at: www.urbaneducator.org

Email: info@urbaneducator.org
Published By: Averie Hatton

- POSITIVITY CAN CHANGE YOUR VIBE.
- I AM MORE THAN ENOUGH.
- TODAY IS A GREAT DAY!
- GOD HAS NOT FORGOTTEN ABOUT YOU.
- YOU ARE AMAZING!
- I CAN DO ALL THINGS THROUGH CHRIST.
- I AM FEARFULLY AND WONDERFULLY MADE.
- I am strong. I am kind.
- I own my magic.
- I'M STRONG, I'M SMART, I'M CAPABLE.
- YOU ARE BEAUTIFUL!
- I AM KIND TO MYSELF.
- No weapon formed against me can prosper.
- I'M BLESSED AND HIGHLY FAVORED.
- I HAVE NO REASON TO FEAR.
- YOU ARE NOT ALONE!

Urban Woman's Annual Journal

No Resolutions, Just Evolution.

We make the same resolutions every year. We want to lose weight. We want to change jobs. We want a better relationship with God. We vow to save money. We plan to travel. We vow to continue our education. However, we are usually back in our regular routines by March.

Why? It starts with belief. Do you really believe you can make a change? All change is temporary without the help of the Father. Let's develop a consistent life of prayer and devotion and God will do the rest.

Proverbs 3:6 King James Version (KJV)
6 In all thy ways acknowledge him, and he shall direct thy paths.

How do I control my physical and emotional urges? If we are continuously overspending, overeating, overthinking, overextending, and/or overriding the voice within, we have to make changes in the form of reachable short-term goals.

Romans 12:1-2 King James Version (KJV)
12 I beseech you therefore, brethren, by the mercies of God, that ye present your bodies a living sacrifice, holy, acceptable unto God, which is your reasonable service.

Please link in with other Urban Sisters. We are forming accountability groups so we can support each other as we walk out our destiny.

I am evolving into everything God intended me to be.

-*Averie Hatton*

Urban Woman's Prayer

PREPARE YOUR HEART. PREPARE YOUR MIND. GOD HAS PREPARED YOU FOR THIS TIME.

A New Year's Prayer

Lord, You make all things new. You bring hope alive in our hearts and cause our spirits to be born again. Thank you for this new year and for all the potential it holds. Come and kindle in us a mighty flame so that in our time many will see the wonders of God and live forever to praise your glorious name. Amen.

Almighty and eternal God, so draw our hearts to thee, so guide our minds, so fill our imaginations, so control our wills, that we may be wholly thine, utterly dedicated unto thee; and then use us, we pray thee, as thou wilt, and always to thy glory and the welfare of thy people; through our Lord and Savior Jesus Christ. Amen.

-Amen

WEEK ONE: 1

January

2 Corinthians 5:17 ESV
"Therefore, if anyone is in Christ, he is a new creation. The old has passed away; behold, the new has come."

WEEK TWO: 2

***Isaiah 43: 18-19** (ESV)*
"Remember not the former things, nor consider the things of old. Behold, I am doing a new thing; now it springs forth, do you not perceive it? I will make a way in the wilderness and rivers in the desert."

There's a song that says, "It's a new season, it's a new day, a fresh anointing is coming your way."
Sis, you don't have to wait on a new year to claim a new season. It may be the new year, but if you need a new beginning today, you can ask for it and receive it. What's new about you? What needs to be renewed?

_____
_____
_____
_____
_____
_____
_____
_____
_____
_____
_____
_____
_____
_____
_____
_____
_____
_____
_____
_____
_____
_____
_____
_____

WEEK THREE: 3

Isaiah 65:17 (NIV)
*"See, I will create new heavens and a new earth. The former things will not be remembered, nor will they come to mind.
You don't have to worry about the old things that we can't seem to forgive ourselves for. God has thrown those things into the sea of forgiveness and they will never return."*

What negative self-perceptions do you need to throw into the sea of forgiveness? Who do you need to forgive as God has forgiven you?

_____
_____
_____
_____
_____
_____
_____
_____
_____
_____
_____
_____
_____
_____
_____
_____
_____
_____
_____
_____
_____
_____
_____
_____
_____
_____
_____

WEEK FOUR: 4

1 Peter 1:3 (ESV)
"Blessed be the God and Father of our Lord Jesus Christ! According to his great mercy, he has caused us to be born again to a living hope through the resurrection of Jesus Christ from the dead..."

We are born again to a living hope. We are resurrecting our hopes and dreams that need to be born again. As long as there is life, there is hope. Do you need to go back and pick up that thing you allowed to be buried? Lord, please let it be born again to a living hope.

WEEK FIVE: 5

Ezekiel 36:26 (ESV)
"And I will give you a new heart, and a new spirit I will put within you. And I will remove the heart of stone from your flesh and give you a heart of flesh."

There are some things we can't do on our own. We need help from God. Sometimes we will forgive everyone else but ourselves. Start the stony heart removal by forgiving yourself first. This is a new year and it's a new you! What are you throwing in the sea of forgiveness this week?

___
___
___
___
___
___
___
___
___
___
___
___
___
___
___
___
___
___
___
___
___
___
___
___
___
___
___
___
___
___

WEEK ONE: 1

THE MONTH OF LOVE……..

John 3:16 (ESV)
"For God so loved the world, that he gave his only Son, that whoever believes in him should not perish but have eternal life."

Psalm 86:15 (ESV)
"But you, O Lord, are a God merciful and gracious, slow to anger and abounding in steadfast love and faithfulness."

1 John 4:8 (ESV)
"Anyone who does not love does not know God, because God is love."

1 John 4:7-8
"Beloved, let us love one another, for love is from God, and whoever loves has been born of God and knows God. 8 Anyone who does not love does not know God, because God is love."

1 Corinthians 13:13 (ESV)
"So now faith, hope, and love abide, these three; but the greatest of these is love."

WEEK ONE: 1

1 John 4:7 (KJV)
"Beloved, let us love one another: for love is of God; and every one that loveth is born of God, and knoweth God."

Love is an action word. I would rather someone show me love than tell me they love me. We want and need to feel loved. In what ways can we show and share the love of Jesus Christ with the world this week?

WEEK TWO: 2

Romans 8:38-39 (KJV)
"For I am persuaded, that neither death, nor life, nor angels, nor principalities, nor powers, nor things present, nor things to come, nor height, nor depth, nor any other creature, shall be able to separate us from the love of God, which is in Christ Jesus our Lord."

I can remember times when I have felt the love of Jesus Christ and I knew it was him and only him that could do the things for me that were done. God's love for us is unconditional. My heavenly Father is always there for me. I want to see myself as he sees me. Reflect on an instance when you know it was no one but God that saw you through. This journal entry should express your love to him.

_____
_____
_____
_____
_____
_____
_____
_____
_____
_____
_____
_____
_____
_____
_____
_____
_____
_____
_____
_____
_____
_____
_____

WEEK THREE: 3

Ephesians 5:25 (KJV)
"Husbands, love your wives, even as Christ also loved the church, and gave himself for it..."

What would happen if we loved each other as Christ loved the church? Forgiveness wouldn't be so hard, and we would love freely. What's your definition of real love? Are you open to receiving that love?

WEEK FOUR: 4

1 John 4:8 (KJV)
"He that loveth not knoweth not God; for God is love."

You may have been exposed to God, but you can't truly know God, our Father without experiencing the love of God. It is through his love and mercy that we are not consumed. This is the month of love. How are you showing love towards your family and friends this week?

_____
_____
_____
_____
_____
_____
_____
_____
_____
_____
_____
_____
_____
_____
_____
_____
_____
_____
_____
_____
_____
_____
_____
_____
_____
_____
_____
_____
_____

WEEK ONE: 1

March

Jeremiah 29:11
"For I know the plans I have for you," declares the LORD, "plans to prosper you and not to harm you, plans to give you hope and a future."

We all have plans for our lives. Does your plan line up with God's plan? God's plan is one of prosperity, hope and a future. How do you know your plan and his plan are one in the same? If it's not, what are you doing to get in line with God's plan?

WEEK TWO: 2

March

Proverbs 3: 5-6
"Trust in the Lord with all your heart and lean not on your own understanding; in all your ways submit to him, and he will make your paths straight."

Circumstances cause us to struggle with trust. Some of us don't trust anyone. Trusting in God is a requirement. You can't walk into your destiny without trusting him. Ask God to show and teach you how to trust him and others. What would have to happen for a person to prove their trust?

WEEK THREE: 3

March

Hebrews 10:36
"You need to persevere so that when you have done the will of God, you will receive what he has promised."

Sister, keep pressing. I know it gets hard sometimes but trust in God and the process. Keep your head up. We are in this together and you will come out as pure gold. Re-affirm yourself today. You're more than a conqueror.

WEEK FOUR: 4

March

Philippians 4:12-13 (NIV)
"I know what it is to be in need, and I know what it is to have plenty. I have learned the secret of being content in any and every situation, whether well fed or hungry, whether living in plenty or in want. I can do all this through him who gives me strength."

Let's take the time to be grateful. I can be content in any state I am in because God knows and sees me. I know he cares for me and I can cast all my cares on him. What cares are you giving to God today?

_____
_____
_____
_____
_____
_____
_____
_____
_____
_____
_____
_____
_____
_____
_____
_____
_____
_____
_____
_____
_____
_____
_____
_____

WEEK ONE: 1

April

John 11:25-26 (NIV)
"Jesus said to her, "I am the resurrection and the life. The one who believes in me will live, even though they die; and whoever lives by believing in me will never die. Do you believe this?"

As we begin to reflect on the love of Jesus Christ and how he gave his life for us, how are you planning to honor him with your life?

_____
_____
_____
_____
_____
_____
_____
_____
_____
_____
_____
_____
_____
_____
_____
_____
_____
_____
_____
_____
_____
_____
_____
_____
_____
_____
_____
_____
_____
_____

WEEK TWO: 2

1 Peter 1:3
"Praise be to the God and Father of our Lord Jesus Christ! In his great mercy he has given us new birth into a living hope through the resurrection of Jesus Christ from the dead."

Christ has given us new birth and hope. I will praise him for his sacrifice. It is because of his sacrifice on the cross that I am living and prospering. I want my life to be an example of God's goodness. Whose life are you impacting and imparting into today?

WEEK THREE: 3

April

Matthew 28:5-6 (NIV)
"The angel said to the women, "Do not be afraid, for I know that you are looking for Jesus, who was crucified. He is not here; he has risen, just as he said. Come and see the place where he lay."

Do not be afraid to live the life Jesus wants you to live. I am committed to facing my fears because I know I have no reason to fear. False. Evidence. Appearing. Real. (F.E.A.R.) It's not real sisters. It's a distraction. Move forward with confidence.

WEEK FOUR: 4

April

Philippians 3:10
"I want to know Christ—yes, to know the power of his resurrection and participation in his sufferings, becoming like him in his death."

We should all strive to have a personal relationship with Christ. If we seek his face, we are the recipients of what's in his hand. During this resurrection month, I am focusing on my relationship with Christ and how it can be strengthened. What are some small things you can do to strengthen your relationship with Christ?

WEEK ONE: 1

Philippians 4:6 (NIV)
"Do not be anxious about anything, but in every situation, by prayer and petition, with thanksgiving, present your requests to God."

Life can present situations that may cause anxiety. However, we don't have to be anxious or afraid. We have an advocate that handles all of our problems. Relax and trust God. Ask him what unnecessary tasks are on your plate and eliminate them. Whatever those things are, let them go so you can be at peace.

_____
_____
_____
_____
_____
_____
_____
_____
_____
_____
_____
_____
_____
_____
_____
_____
_____
_____
_____
_____
_____
_____
_____
_____
_____
_____

WEEK TWO: 2

Psalm 22:19 (NIV)
"But you, Lord, do not be far from me. You are my strength; come quickly to help me."

God is our strength. Any strength we have, it is he who gives. Allow the love of Christ to help you strengthen someone else in need. When you strengthen others, you will obtain the strength you need.

"I am important. I am fearless."

ALL THINGS WORK TOGETHER FOR THE GOOD OF THEM THAT LOVE THE LORD.

GOD WILL MAKE MY ENEMIES MY FOOTSTOOL.

I am dope, I am amazing, I am confident, I am secure, I am loved.

MOVE IN SILENCE.

GOD IS MY SOURCE.

YOU ARE DIFFERENT.

Let my voice speak out with compassion and calm.

I am deliberate and afraid of nothing.

THERE IS NO FAILURE IN GOD.

WEEK THREE: 3

May

John 16:33 (NIV)
"I have told you these things, so that in me you may have peace. In this world you will have trouble. But take heart! I have overcome the world."

Let's take some time to encourage ourselves. There is no situation that you can't overcome. If you need forgiveness, ask for it and keep moving forward. No one is perfect. Keep striving. How are you feeling this week?

WEEK FOUR: 4

Proverbs 18:10 (NIV)
"The name of the Lord is a fortified tower; the righteous run to it and are safe."

What does it mean to feel safe? I feel loved, protected and cared for. I feel freedom to explore the many possibilities and opportunities that come my way. I'm free to give and receive love from people and view all situations through a lens of love.

WEEK ONE: 1

Hebrews 4:8 (NKJV)
"Draw near to God and He will draw near to you. Cleanse your hands, you sinners; and purify your hearts, you double-minded."

Sisters, when you are feeling alone or uncertain of yourself, God is there. The answers we seek are in his presence. When we draw nearer to him, he draws near to us. When God is with and near you, you have no reason to fear. Move forward in confidence. What effort are you making to step out of your comfort zone this week?

_____
_____
_____
_____
_____
_____
_____
_____
_____
_____
_____
_____
_____
_____
_____
_____
_____
_____
_____
_____
_____

WEEK TWO: 2

Psalm 145:18
"The Lord is near to all who call upon Him, to all who call upon Him in truth."

God is near to those who call upon him.
Consistency is key. Continue to call on him and he promises to hear our call. Use your voice. Take a moment to call upon God. Praise and thank him. Watch him work miracles in your life. Can you name a time when you know beyond a doubt it was no one but the Lord that heard your voice and answered your prayer?

WEEK THREE: 3

Luke 9:23 (NKJV)
"Then he said to them all, if anyone desires to come after Me, let him deny himself, and take up the cross daily, and follow Me."

Sisters, we live our lives daily. Every morning we are given new mercies and opportunities. No need to focus on yesterday's negativity. What do you need to give to God so you can take up your daily cross? His yoke is easy, and his burden is light.

WEEK FOUR: 4

2 Timothy 2:13
"If we are faithless, He remains faithful; He cannot deny Himself."

Sisters, we have to help one another build faith. Certain situations can render us faithless at times. Never forget God is on your side. You can make it! Encourage yourself in the Lord. God is faithful and his plan is not for you to be denied.

WEEK ONE: 1

John 8:36
"If the Son therefore shall make you free, ye shall be free indeed. Who the son sets free is free indeed."

Sister, walk in freedom. Freedom from negativity and people who don't want you to be free. Affirm yourself. Your freedom in Christ shines like a light in darkness. Continue to be the light.

WEEK TWO: 2

July

Romans 8:2

"For the law of the Spirit of life in Christ Jesus hath made me free from the law of sin and death."

We celebrate freedom this week. I am grateful that I am free, and I choose to lead others to freedom. Live your life as God has shown you. Live outside of the world's box. Grab your sister by the hand and take her with you.

WEEK THREE: 3

July

Galatians 5:13 (NIV)

"You, my brothers and sisters, were called to be free. But do not use your freedom to indulge the flesh; rather, serve one another humbly in love."

Humility is the best way to live. No matter how far we go in life, we didn't get here on our own. We had help and we should reach back and help someone else. How are you helping to build the next generation?

_____
_____
_____
_____
_____
_____
_____
_____
_____
_____
_____
_____
_____
_____
_____
_____
_____
_____
_____
_____
_____
_____
_____
_____
_____

WEEK FOUR: 4

Revelation 1:5-6 (NRSV)
"…and from Jesus Christ, the faithful witness, the firstborn of the dead, and the ruler of the kings of the earth. To him who loves us and freed us from our sins by his blood, and made us to be a kingdom, priests serving his God and Father, to him be glory and dominion forever and ever. Amen."

Sisters, rest in the knowledge that we are loved. We must learn to love ourselves as the Father loves us. We all have areas we need to work on, but we are worthy of and deserve love. What are you doing to show self love this week?

WEEK ONE: 1

August

Mark 11:25 (NIV)
"And when you stand praying, if you hold anything against anyone, forgive them, so that your Father in heaven may forgive you your sins."

Forgiveness is for you. When we forgive, we release ourselves from the actions of others that have had a negative impact on our lives. We can only control our own actions. God can handle people much better than we can. Take a moment to mentally release some people. You need the headspace to do great things!

WEEK TWO: 2

August

Matthew 6:14-15 (NIV)
"For if you forgive other people when they sin against you, your heavenly Father will also forgive you. But if you do not forgive others their sins, your Father will not forgive your sins."

Sister, you will be much happier when you learn to forgive. God has a built-in reward system in place. When we forgive, God forgives us. Thank you, Lord, for forgiveness. I do not take anything for granted.

WEEK THREE: 3

August

Titus 1:8 (KJV)
"But a lover of hospitality, a lover of good men, sober, just, holy, temperate."

Father, we thank you for another year. We start off this year with a deeper understanding of who you are in my life. I realize I don't have to fight my own battles. You are going to fight for me. If I don't see immediate change, I am temperate and patient waiting on you. Not my will but your will be done. What things are you holding on to that you need to place in God's hands? Release yourself from the pressure and let God be God.

_____
_____
_____
_____
_____
_____
_____
_____
_____
_____
_____
_____
_____
_____
_____
_____
_____
_____
_____
_____
_____
_____
_____

WEEK FOUR: 4

August

Matthew 26:41 (NIV)
"Watch and pray so that you will not fall into temptation. The spirit is willing, but the flesh is weak."

Let's not forget the enemy will tempt us when we attempt to make positive changes in our lives. Stay strong in your devotion and prayer life. You will find the strength you need to get past temptation one day at a time. You're not in this alone. We are here to support one another.

Can people call on you for support? What are your strengths? In what areas do you need the most support?

WEEK ONE: 1

September

Lamentations 3:22 (NIV)
"Because of the Lord's great love we are not consumed, for his compassions never fail. They are new every morning; great is your faithfulness."

Lord we thank you that you love us so much that you will not allow us to be consumed. You give us new mercies every day. Great is your faithfulness towards me. I am grateful and I don't take your love, compassion or mercy for granted. What small things can you focus on that allow you to be grateful while you wait and work towards your destiny?

_____
_____
_____
_____
_____
_____
_____
_____
_____
_____
_____
_____
_____
_____
_____
_____
_____
_____
_____
_____

WEEK TWO: 2

September

Ecclesiastes 3:11 (NIV)
"He has made everything beautiful in its time. He has also set eternity in the human heart; yet[a] no one can fathom what God has done from beginning to end."

God is in control of everything. Even when we are out of control and things seem out of control, God has not and will not move. Claim your peace and move in God's timing. What person or thing do you need to place in God's hands? It is not his will that you be frustrated. Pray more.

WEEK THREE: 3

September

Ephesians 6:11 (NIV)
"Put on the full armor of God, so that you can take your stand against the devil's schemes."

Sisters, we have to take care of ourselves. Your emotional, physical and mental state of being may cause you to be weak and therefore, you don't display your full armor. How are you showing self love this week? Build your armor so you can stand.

WEEK FOUR: 4

September

James 1:12 (NIV)
"Blessed is the one who perseveres under trial because, having stood the test, that person will receive the crown of life that the Lord has promised to those who love him."

Sisters, we are overcomers. We have been through many test and come out as pure gold! Take a moment to reflect on the things you've been through and you're still here! People may see your glory, but they don't know your real story. You're more than a conqueror.

WEEK ONE: 1

Galatians 6:9 (NIV)
"Let us not become weary in doing good, for at the proper time we will reap a harvest if we do not give up."

Sister, I know you may feel tired, but this is not the time to give up. We have a promise that good things are coming to those of us who are waiting. Celebrate others because our victories are on the way! Make a list of what you're waiting on and begin to give thanks because it is on the way!

WEEK TWO: 2

Hebrews 12:1 (NIV)
"Therefore, since we are surrounded by such a great cloud of witnesses, let us throw off everything that hinders and the sin that so easily entangles. And let us run with perseverance the race marked out for us..."

Sisters, don't let the small things throw you off. Others before us have successfully ran the course. So can we! I refuse to let small distractions keep me from my destiny. Elevate your thinking and your expectations of yourself.

WEEK THREE: 3

James 1:2-4 (NIV)
"Consider it pure joy, my brothers and sisters,[a] whenever you face trials of many kinds, 3 because you know that the testing of your faith produces perseverance. 4 Let perseverance finish its work so that you may be mature and complete, not lacking anything."

The joy of the Lord is my strength. Sister, guard your joy as if your life depends on it. Your joy can't be emotional. It's a conscious decision to be joyous. Your joy is infectious, and others are counting on it.

WEEK FOUR: 4

Philippians 1:6 (NIV)
"Being confident of this, that he who began a good work in you will carry it on to completion until the day of Christ Jesus."

Sometimes we start to look at our age and what others have accomplished. Sister, the God we serve is not looking at our age and what others have done. He still has a plan for our lives, and he will bring us to that expected end. Today, I encourage myself. If I'm on a different route, Lord please reveal your good work in me.

WEEK ONE: 1

Deut. 20:4
"For the Lord your God is the one who goes with you to fight for you against your enemies to give you victory."

Sister, you don't have to fight. God fights our battles. It may not be the immediate gratification we seek. However, when God fights it's a guaranteed victory. We can rest. God knows and sees all. I'm so glad he's in control. Breathe in the good vibes and release any negativity. How are you loving yourself this week?

WEEK TWO: 2

Joshua 1:9

"Have I not commanded you? Be strong and courageous. Do not be afraid; do not be discouraged, for the LORD your God will be with you wherever you go."

Wherever you go, you are not alone. God is there to help us be strong and courageous. Sister, go ahead and take the next step forward. You may be afraid, but God is with you wherever you go.

WEEK THREE: 3

1 Chronicles 16:34-35
"Oh give thanks to the Lord, for he is good; for his steadfast love endures forever! Say also: Save us, O God of our salvation, and gather and deliver us from among the nations, that we may give thanks to your holy name and glory in your praise."

Sister, today is a day of Thanksgiving! We take a moment to thank God for all he's done for us and our family. There are many that have gone on before us. It could have been us, but God has spared our lives and he has given us another chance. What small things are you grateful for this week?

_____
_____
_____
_____
_____
_____
_____
_____
_____
_____
_____
_____
_____
_____
_____
_____
_____
_____
_____
_____
_____
_____
_____
_____

WEEK FOUR: 4

Psalm 7:17
"I will give to the Lord the thanks due to his righteousness, and I will sing praise to the name of the Lord, the Most High."

We have so much to be thankful for. I am thankful that God has strengthened me and am confident that I'm going to walk out my destiny. I'm moving toward my wealthy place on a daily basis. I am the lender and not the borrower. God made me the head and not the tail. I am also a servant and I'm committed to uplifting all that are around me.

WEEK ONE: 1

December

1 Corinthians 9:24-27 (NIV)

"Do you not know that in a race all the runners run, but only one gets the prize? Run in such a way as to get the prize. 25 Everyone who competes in the games goes into strict training. They do it to get a crown that will not last, but we do it to get a crown that will last forever. 26 Therefore I do not run like someone running aimlessly; I do not fight like a boxer beating the air. 27 No, I strike a blow to my body and make it my slave so that after I have preached to others, I myself will not be disqualified for the prize."

Sister, run the race strategically.
Sometimes you have to move in silence. Keep praying. Seek God for direction and run YOUR race. When we focus on our race, we encourage others around us to do the same. Wouldn't it be wonderful if we all made it? There's room for everyone.

WEEK TWO: 2

Jeremiah 32:27 (NIV)
"I am the Lord, the God of all mankind. Is anything too hard for me?"

There is nothing too hard for God. There are some things we can't handle. We have to turn it over to God. It builds our faith and trust in him. He will never let us down.

WEEK THREE: 3

1 Corinthians 9:24 (NIV)
"Do you not know that in a race all the runners run, but only one gets the prize? Run in such a way as to get the prize."

We've been running this race for an entire year. We made it! I'm confident that I am running with a specific destination in mind. God didn't bring me this far to leave me. I'm looking to go to higher heights and deeper depths. This next year will be my next year.

WEEK FOUR: 4

Romans 8:29 (NIV)
"For those God foreknew he also predestined to be conformed to the image of his Son, that he might be the firstborn among many brothers and sisters."

I am predestined. God has a plan for my life and all I have to do is follow his lead. God has given me great ideas and I am determined to live the life God has planned for me. When I go to heaven, I will have fulfilled my destiny here on earth. I will not die unfulfilled.

NOTES:

NOTES:

NOTES:

NOTES:

NOTES:

NOTES:

NOTES:

NOTES:

NOTES:

"I Can Do It Too" Averie Hatton
Print Length: 29 pages
Publisher: Page Publishing, Inc. (March 13, 2019)
Publication Date: March 13, 2019
Sold by: Amazon Digital Services LLC
Language: English
ISBN: 978-1-64082-016-6

Now Available at www.averiefoundation.org
or www.amazon.com

www.ingramcontent.com/pod-product-compliance
Lightning Source LLC
Chambersburg PA
CBHW040015240426
43664CB00036B/9